W9-CIH-774

GOLD
MEDAL
GAMES

SPORTS
OF THE
PARALYMPIC GAMES

Aaron Derr

RED
CHAIR
•PRESS•

Gold Medal Games is produced and published by Red Chair Press:

Red Chair Press LLC   PO Box 333   South Egremont, MA 01258-0333

www.redchairpress.com

Publisher's Cataloging-In-Publication Data

Names: Derr, Aaron, author. | Sperling, Thomas, 1952- illustrator.

Title: Sports of the Paralympic Games / Aaron Derr ; [illustrations by
    Thomas Sperling].

Description: South Egremont, MA : Red Chair Press, [2020] | Series: Gold
    medal games | Interest age level: 007-010. | Includes bibliographical
    references and index. | Summary: "An overview of the Paralympic Games
    featuring sports played by Individuals and teams of athletes competing
    against each other ... Like the Olympic Games, the Paralympic Games
    showcase super strength and skills, stamina and endurance both
    individually and through teamwork."--Provided by publisher.

Identifiers: ISBN 9781634407243 (library hardcover) | ISBN 9781634407298
    (paperback) | ISBN 9781634407342 (ebook)

Subjects: LCSH: Paralympic Games--Juvenile literature. | Sports for people
    with disabilities--Juvenile literature. | CYAC: Paralympic Games. |
    Sports for people with disabilities.

Classification: LCC GV722.5.P37 D47 2020 (print) | LCC GV722.5.P37 (ebook)
    | DDC 796.087--dc23

LCCN: 2018963387

Photo credits: Cover (top), p. 31 © Xinhua/Alamy; cover (left), pp. 1, 3, 18,
24–29, 32, 35, 40, 42–43 Shutterstock; cover (right), pp. 19, 41 © Aflo Co.
Ltd./Alamy; pp. 4, 5 © History and Art Collection/Alamy; pp. 7, 8, 9 © Trinity
Mirror/Mirrorpix/Alamy; p. 10 © PA Images/Alamy; p. 11 © Bob Thomas/
Getty Images; p. 12 © Heinz Kluetmeier/Getty Images; pp. 14, 20, 22, 36 © dpa
picture alliance archive/Alamy; p. 15 © Bruna Prado/Getty Images; pp. 16,
23, 33 © PhotoAbility/Alamy; pp. 17, 30, 45 © Bob Daemmrich/Alamy; p. 21 ©
Scott Barbour/Getty Images; p. 34 © Action Plus Sports Images/Alamy; p. 37 ©
Marco Ciccolella/Alamy; p. 38 © /Getty Images; p. 39 © Jamie McDonald/Getty
Images; p. 44 © ZUMA Press, Inc./Alamy; p. 47 © Mark Davidson/Alamy.

Printed in the United States of America

0619 1P CGS20

TABLE OF CONTENTS

THE PARALYMPIC GAMES

George Eyser (center both photos) in gymnastics
competition, Frankfurt, Germany, 1908.

George Eyser had a lot of success at the 1904 Summer Olympics. The American gymnast won six medals on the same day! But Eyser was different than all of the other Olympic athletes in one important way.

When Eyser was a boy growing up in St. Louis, Missouri, he injured his leg so badly that doctors had to remove it completely. They replaced it with an artificial limb, called a prosthesis. Eyser's wooden leg allowed him to run and play with the other boys.

In 1904, Eyser became the first athlete with a disability to compete in the Olympic Games.

Over the years, more and more athletes with a range of disabilities began to excel in a variety of sports. It wouldn't be long before disabled athletes earned their own Olympic Games.

In 1948, the Stoke Mandeville Games for the **Paralyzed** became the first official set of events open only to disabled athletes. It was special because it took place alongside the 1948 Olympic Games in the United Kingdom. The event was named after the Stoke Mandeville Hospital in England. The hospital was the first to include a special center for people who had suffered spinal injuries.

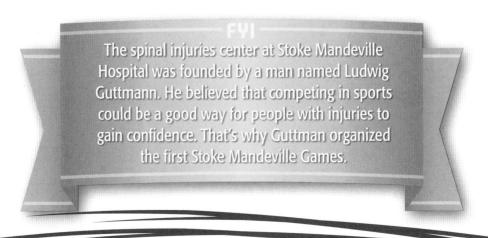

FYI

The spinal injuries center at Stoke Mandeville Hospital was founded by a man named Ludwig Guttmann. He believed that competing in sports could be a good way for people with injuries to gain confidence. That's why Guttman organized the first Stoke Mandeville Games.

200 men and women in wheelchairs competed at the 1948 Stoke Mandeville Games.

An athlete trains before the 1964 Stoke Mandeville Games held in Tokyo.

The Stoke Mandeville Games involved 16 injured British war **veterans**—14 men and two women—who took part in **archery**. It was an important **milestone** for people with disabilities.

In 1952, a team from Netherlands participated in the Stoke Mandeville Games. Because it now included athletes from more than one country, the event was called the 1st International Stoke Mandeville Games. More and more athletes from around the world joined the competition in the following years.

Engineers at Stoke Mandeville prepare equipment for athletes in 1964.

More than Wheelchairs

The 1960 Games were held in Rome. It featured 400 disabled athletes from 23 different countries. It was really growing fast! Back then, the Games were often referred to as the Wheelchair Olympics, because they were only open to athletes in wheelchairs.

England's Diane Gubbin won one Silver and two Bronze medals while her fiance Dick Thompson won four Gold medals at the 1960 Games in Rome.

New Zealand's Neroli Fairhall competes in women's archery.

That changed in 1976, when athletes with different disabilities were included. That year, the Games featured 1,600 athletes from 40 different countries. For the first time, the Games were called the Paralympics. The word is a combination of the words paraplegic—a person affected by paralysis of the lower body—and Olympics.

USA's Craig Blanchette leads the
1500m wheelchair race, 1988, Seoul.

By 1988, the Paralympics were so popular
that they were held immediately after the
Summer Games. The Paralympic athletes even
used the same **facilities** used by the athletes in
the Summer Olympics. Now, there are Summer
Paralympic Games and Winter Paralympic Games.

The word Paralympics has a second meaning. The Greek word *pará* means "alongside." The Paralympics now happen *alongside* the Olympic Games. The Paralympics help people realize that a person with a disability can also be a special athlete just like a fully able person.

"The Paralympic Games actually turned my whole **mentality** around about disability," says Lee Pearson, an 11-time Paralympic Games gold medalist. "When you're in the Paralympic Games and there are 4,000 disabled people, you stop seeing disability."

Gold Medal Cities

The Paralympic Games are hosted by different cities just like the Olympic Games. Here is a list of the host cities for the most recent Paralympic Games, plus some that haven't even happened yet!

2022: Beijing	2012: London	2002: Salt Lake City
2020: Tokyo	2010: Vancouver	2000: Sydney
2018: PyeongChang	2008: Beijing	1998: Nagano
2016: Rio de Janeiro	2006: Turin	1996: Atlanta
2014: Sochi	2004: Athens	1994: Lillehammer

CHAPTER
2

INDIVIDUAL SPORTS AT THE SUMMER PARALYMPICS

China's Jinzhi Li in archery competition, 2012 London games.

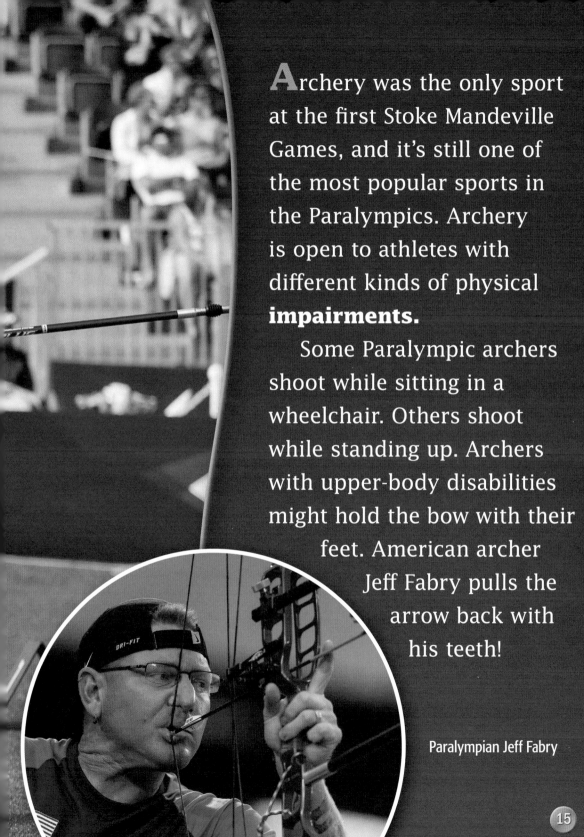

Archery was the only sport at the first Stoke Mandeville Games, and it's still one of the most popular sports in the Paralympics. Archery is open to athletes with different kinds of physical **impairments.**

Some Paralympic archers shoot while sitting in a wheelchair. Others shoot while standing up. Archers with upper-body disabilities might hold the bow with their feet. American archer Jeff Fabry pulls the arrow back with his teeth!

Paralympian Jeff Fabry

Fabry was injured in a motorcycle accident when he was 15. Doctors had to remove his right arm at the elbow and his right leg above the knee. He competes in archery using the same kind of bow that everyone else uses.

"The only difference is the mouth tab on the string," Fabry says.

Even though he's been competing in Paralympic archery for 13 years, his dentist says it doesn't seem to be doing any damage to his teeth.

In the Paralympic **athletics** competition, athletes participate in short races, medium races, long races and relay races. They also do shot put, high jump and discus throw. Most of the rules are the same as the rules for able-bodied competitors.

Germany's Vanessa Low sets a Long Jump world record in the 2016 Rio games.

The Paralympic Games are open to athletes who have a physical impairment, visual impairment or **intellectual** disability.

USA's David Brown and guide Jerome Avery (r) win the 200m heat at the 2016 Rio games.

17

Johannes Floors of Germany (r)
running the 100m race in Rio, 2016.

Disabled; Not Unabled

Johannes Floors is a Para athlete from Germany. He had his feet **amputated** when he was 16 years old. But he didn't slow down. In fact, he got faster.

"I just wanted to show others what is possible with prosthetic legs," Floors says.

Many Paralympic runners use prosthetics called running blades. They look like curved skis. They aren't made for walking, but when Paralympic athletes put them on for a race, they can really fly!

"I wasn't able to run properly for 16 years," Floors says. "Then there is someone giving you the opportunity to run. To feel wind. To feel speed. It's an amazing feeling."

Athletes who use wheelchairs can compete in **fencing** and tennis. Even though the athletes are sitting the entire time, the rules are basically the same as they are for able-bodied athletes.

Japan's Yui Kamiji, won the Women's singles Bronze medal, Rio 2016.

The Greatest

Most Paralympic athletes are split into groups based on the type and extent of their disability. This allows athletes to compete against other athletes with similar abilities. Swimmers, for example, are assigned a category between 1 and 10. Physical disabilities of swimmers might include the loss of an arm or leg, **spinal cord** injuries, **dwarfism** or **cerebral palsy**.

Athletes start the Men's 50m Butterfly Finals, Rio 2016.

USA's Trischa Zorn wins Silver in the Women's 100m Breastsroke, Sydney 2000 games.

One of the most successful athletes in the history of the Paralympic Games is Trischa Zorn, a swimmer from the United States. Zorn was born without the ability to see. She went on to win 5 bronze medals, 9 silver medals, and an amazing 41 gold medals!

"It was a platform for all athletes to show their abilities, not their disabilities," Zorn says. "Athletes respected one another and cheered one another on during all competitions."

Germany's Erich Winkler competes in Men's Cycling at Rio de Janeiro, 2016.

Biking All the Way

Para cycling was developed in the 1980s. Back then, it was only for visually impaired athletes. The cyclists would compete on a two-person bike with a sighted partner.

Nowadays, Paralympic cycling includes events on a track and a road and is open to cyclists with various disabilities. Athletes might compete on bicycles, or they might ride tricycles or hand cycles, which are powered by their arms instead of their legs.

There is one individual sport at the Summer Paralympic Games that does not have an Olympic sport with the same name. Boccia (pronounced *botch-ya*) is for athletes with impairments that affect **motor skills**. Players throw, roll or kick a series of blue and red balls at a white target ball. The player with the most balls closest to the target ball is the winner.

Boccia bronze medal; game, Rio 2016.

TEAM SPORTS AT THE SUMMER PARALYMPIC GAMES

Brazil and Argentina face off in 2016, Rio de Janeiro. USA won gold in these games.

CHAPTER 3

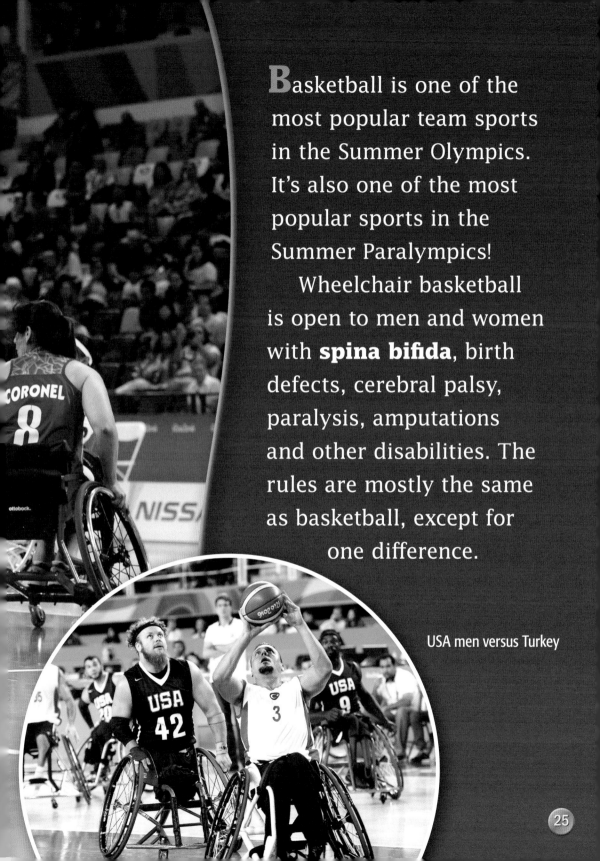

Basketball is one of the most popular team sports in the Summer Olympics. It's also one of the most popular sports in the Summer Paralympics!

Wheelchair basketball is open to men and women with **spina bifida**, birth defects, cerebral palsy, paralysis, amputations and other disabilities. The rules are mostly the same as basketball, except for one difference.

USA men versus Turkey

In the NBA, a player is called for "traveling" if he takes more than two steps without passing, shooting or coming to a stop. In wheelchair basketball, traveling occurs when the athlete touches their wheels more than twice after receiving the ball.

Basketball wheelchairs have lower seats and slanted wheels so they are less likely to tip over.

Traveling is when wheels bump more than two times in one possession.

A Fun Version of Soccer

Football 5-a-side is a version of *football* (In America, we call it *soccer*!) for athletes with visual impairments. The field is smaller and surrounded by boards. Teams have five players each, including a goalie. Each team also uses guides, who stand off to the side and shout instructions to players so they know which way to go.

Teams from Brazil and China compete in the men's 5-a-side, Rio, 2016.

But the most unusual thing about football 5-a-side is the ball, which has a sound system inside it so the players can tell where it is. Because of this, fans at football 5-a-side matches must stay super quiet so the players can hear the ball!

Volleyball Without Wheelchairs

In Paralympic volleyball—also called sitting volleyball—players don't use wheelchairs. Instead, they remain in a seated position on the floor during the entire game. The court is smaller and the net is lower than in stand-up volleyball, making for some exciting, fast-paced action.

After one team serves, the other team has three chances to tap the ball back over the net before it touches the ground. Players will often **lunge** and dive to keep the ball alive!

The women's team from China won gold medals in the 2004, 2008 and 2012 Paralympic Games, but the U.S. team finally broke through with a gold medal in 2016. It was a surprising **upset**!

USA versus Iran,
Women's volleyball, 2016

The two best teams in Women's Volleyball, China and the United States, compete in Rio, 2016.

Smash!

One of the most intense sports in all of the Paralympics is wheelchair rugby. While **rugby football** is generally played outside on grass, wheelchair rugby is played on an indoor court, similar to basketball.

Brazil versus Canada, in 2016, Rio de Janeiro.

Rugby match, 2016, Brazil versus Canada.

But unlike basketball, wheelchair rugby is a full-contact sport. Players smash into each other as they try to score the ball—or stop the other team from scoring. It's not unusual for a player to get knocked over in wheelchair rugby, but that's OK! It's all a part of the game!

Goal!

Goalball is a team sport designed for athletes with a vision impairment. It's played on a court like basketball or volleyball. But the game is really more like soccer or handball.

Three players on each side try to throw a ball past their opponents and into the net to score. Unlike soccer, the goals in goalball stretch across the entire end of the court! Similar to football 5-a-side, the ball in goalball makes a noise so athletes can tell where it is. A line of string on the floor helps the players get in the correct position.

Team Turkey beats Lithuania for bronze in Men's Goalball, London 2012.

It's a fast-paced game. If one team stops the other from scoring, they can only hold onto the ball for 10 seconds before throwing or rolling it toward the other goal.

Goalball is like handball for athletes with limited eyesight.
The ball makes a noise so players know where to lunge.

CHAPTER 4

THE WINTER PARALYMPIC GAMES

USA's Mike Schultz wins Gold in Men's Snowboard Cross, 2018 PyeongChang. Shultz was team USA's opening ceremony flagbearer, too.

The Winter Paralympic Games look a lot like the Winter Olympic Games. There's skiing, hockey, curling and snowboarding. But the thing they most have in common is that the athletes work as hard as they can to perform the best that they can!

Great Britain competes in Curling, 2018.

Alpine skiing, also called downhill skiing, has been a popular sport for hundreds of years. Para alpine skiing was originally developed for soldiers who were injured in World War II. Now it's one of the most popular and exciting events in the Paralympic Games.

Disabled skiers shoot down the mountainside with **modified** equipment. An athlete who can't stand could use a chair that's attached to skis. Athletes that have lost a leg use a pole with a small ski attached to the end to help them keep their balance.

Linda van Impelen of Netherlands won Silver in Women's Alpine skiing, 2018 PyeongChang. She skis seated.

Germany's Gerd Schönfelder, competing in the Men's Downhill in Vancouver, 2010. In 2012, he was named best all-sport athlete of Germany.

One of the best para-alpine skiers in history is a man from Germany named Gerd Schönfelder. After losing his right arm in an accident when he was 19, he earned 22 medals in his career.

"Sports are good for everyone," Schönfelder says. "But for people with disabilities, it is even more important. It is the perfect way to get more out of yourself, to gain quality of life and become more independent."

Skiing Cross Country

Paralympic skiers can also compete in cross-country skiing. Instead of flying down a hill, cross-country skiers have to work hard to move

Sitting Cross-country skiers

across flat ground. Sometimes they even ski uphill!

Standing Paralympic cross-country skiers might have arm or leg impairments. Cross-country skiers with severe leg impairments might sit in a chair. They have to be super strong to push themselves across the snow using only their arms.

Cross-country skiers can also compete in the biathlon, which combines skiing with rifle shooting. Visually impaired skiers use a rifle that makes a noise so they can tell where they are aiming.

FYI

The International Paralympic Committee has considered adding the sport of bobsleigh to the Winter Paralympics. Bobsleigh—sometimes called bobsled—is a sport where drivers steer a sled down an icy track at high speeds. It's super exciting!

Snowboarding is a lot like skiing, except the athletes use a board similar in size to a skateboard instead of a pair of skis. Athletes with impairments in one or both legs can compete sitting down. Athletes with impairments affecting their arms can stand up.

There are also **classifications** for competitors who are deaf or blind or have intellectual disabilities.

Paralympic snowboarders zoom down the slope in several different races. They might have to twist around tight turns or fly over jumps. One thing's for sure: They always go fast!

Standing Snowboard athlete.

One of the most interesting sports in the Winter Olympics is Curling. Players take turns pushing stones down a sheet of ice toward a target. Whichever team gets the most stones closest to the target wins.

The object in wheelchair curling is the same, except the stones are thrown from athletes sitting in wheelchairs. Wheelchair curlers can throw the stones with their hands. Or they can use a stick to push the stones down the ice.

If one team gets a lot of stones close to the target, the other team can't give it. That's because they can always throw their own stones to knock the others out of the way!

Team Great Briatain competes in Curling, 2018.

Sled hockey, Italy versus USA, 2018 PyeongChang.

Do You Believe in Miracles?

Para ice hockey, also known as sled hockey, was designed to allow participants with physical disabilities to play the game of ice hockey. Para ice hockey rules are mostly the same, except that Paralympic hockey players sit on sleds and use two sticks instead of one.

The athletes don't only use their sticks to shoot the puck. They also use them to push themselves around the ice on their sleds.

DID YOU KNOW?

Ice sledge racing was a Winter Paralympic sport as recently as 1998. Athletes used poles to push themselves around an ice skating rink in a sledge—more often called a sled or sleigh.

At Sochi 2014 games, Team USA beat Team Russia for Gold in Men's Sled Hockey.

The United States has one of the most successful para ice hockey programs in the history of the Winter Paralympics. Team USA has won four gold medals. No other country has won more than one!

At the 2018 Games in South Korea, things weren't looking good for the U.S. team. Near the end of the game, Canada was winning 1–0. But shockingly, with 37 seconds left, Declan Farmer scored a goal for the USA. The game was tied!

In overtime, Farmer scored again! The USA won the game, and another gold medal.

"It's incredible," Farmer says. "Especially to go to overtime. That's what kids dream of."

Inspiring Stories

For more than 50 years, the Paralympic Games have provided disabled athletes the opportunity to compete in the highest level of their sport.

Some of the athletes were born with their disability. Others were injured in an accident or suffered permanent damage from an illness.

All of them have inspired us all with their bravery, determination and hard work.

We can't wait for the next Paralympic Games!

Disabled or fully-abled, athletes who compete hard are an inspiration to all.

Glossary

amputated an operation to remove a person's arm or leg

archery the sport of shooting a bow and arrow

athletics track and field competition at the Olympics

cerebral palsy a condition that causes impaired muscle use

classifications grouping similar things together

dwarfism unusually small in size

facilities a place used for a special purpose

fencing the sport of fighting with swords

impairments something that is weakened or damaged

intellectual the ability to understand things

lunge to thrust forward with arms outstretched

mentality a way of thinking

milestone an important event

modified something that has been changed

motor skills an action that involves using your muscles

NBA National Basketball Association professional basketball league

paralyzed partially or entirely unable to move

rugby football a team game played with a ball that can be kicked, carried or passed

spina bifida a condition when the spine is defective; it can cause paralysis

spinal cord a important set of nerves that runs up your back

upset an unexpected result in a game

veterans people who have served in the military

FOR MORE INFORMATION

Books

Purdy, Amy. *On My Own Two Feet: From Losing My Legs to Learning the Dance of Life.* William Morrow. 2015.

McFadden, Tatyana. *Ya Sama! Moments from My Life.* Lerner. 2017.

Snyder, Brad. *Fire in My Eyes: An American Warrior's Journey from Being Blinded on the Battlefield to Gold Medal Victory.* Da Capo Press. 2016.

Places

University of Illinois Division of Disability Resources and Educational Services. Champaign, Illinois. U.S. Paralympic Training Site.

Turnstone Center for Adults and Children with Disabilities. Fort Wayne, Indiana. Training site for men's and women's goalball.

Spire Institute. Geneva, Ohio. Training site for wheelchair basketball.

INDEX

ABOUT THE AUTHOR

Aaron Derr is a writer based just outside of Dallas, Texas. He has more than 15 years of experience as a writer and editor for magazines such as *Sports Illustrated for Kids*, *TIME for Kids*, and *Boys Life*. When he's not reading or writing, Aaron enjoys watching and playing sports, and doing pretty much anything with his wife and two kids.